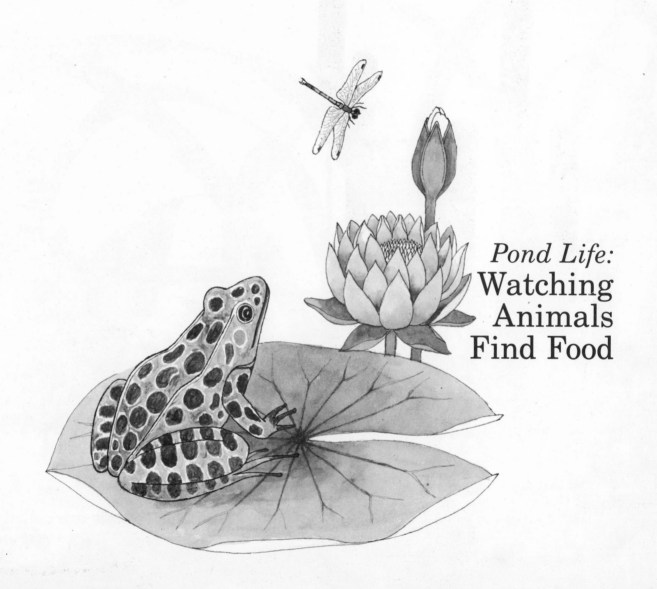

Pond Life:
Watching
Animals
Find Food

Pond Life:

Watching Animals Find Food

*by Herbert H. Wong
and Matthew F. Vessel*

illustrated by Tony Chen

▲ Addison-Wesley

Science Series for the Young

Level A
My Goldfish
My Ladybug
Our Tree
Our Terrariums

Level B:
Pond Life: Watching Animals Find Food
Animal Habitats: Where Can Red-Winged Blackbirds Live?
Plant Communities: Where Can Cattails Grow?
Pond Life: Watching Animals Grow Up

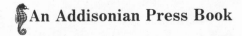 An Addisonian Press Book

Text Copyright © 1970 by Herbert H. Wong and Matthew F. Vessel
Illustrations Copyright © 1970 by Tony Chen
All Rights Reserved
Addison-Wesley Publishing Company, Inc.
Reading, Massachusetts 01867
Library of Congress Card Catalog No. 72-105875
ISBN: 0-201-08732-4
Printed in the United States of America
Second Printing

GO/WZ   5/75   08732

SCIENCE
SERIES
FOR THE
YOUNG

Can we catch fish here?
Yes, I think so.
I can see some little ones.
Dad says there are big ones here, too.

6

Hey! Look at that big bird!
The hawk? Yes, look — it is coming down.
It is going to catch something.

The hawk has a mouse!
What other animals
  does a hawk eat?
Well, maybe we can find out.
Maybe the hawk will catch
  some other animals.

9

The hawk is over the cattails.
What is it after? Blackbirds? A muskrat?
The hawk dives. It comes down fast!

Where did the blackbirds go?
Into the cattails!
The muskrat dives
into the water.
The hawk must look
for other food.

Do all animals have to catch food?
No. Not the ones that eat plants.
Some animals eat just plants.
Some eat animals.
Some eat plants and animals.

Do you see the green plants in the water?
There, by the cattails.
The plants in the water are algae.

There are little animals in the water, too.
Some of the little animals are called daphnia.
The daphnia eat algae.
They eat other things, too.

Does something eat the daphnia?
Yes. There are insects in the water.
These are backswimmers.
The backswimmers eat the daphnia.

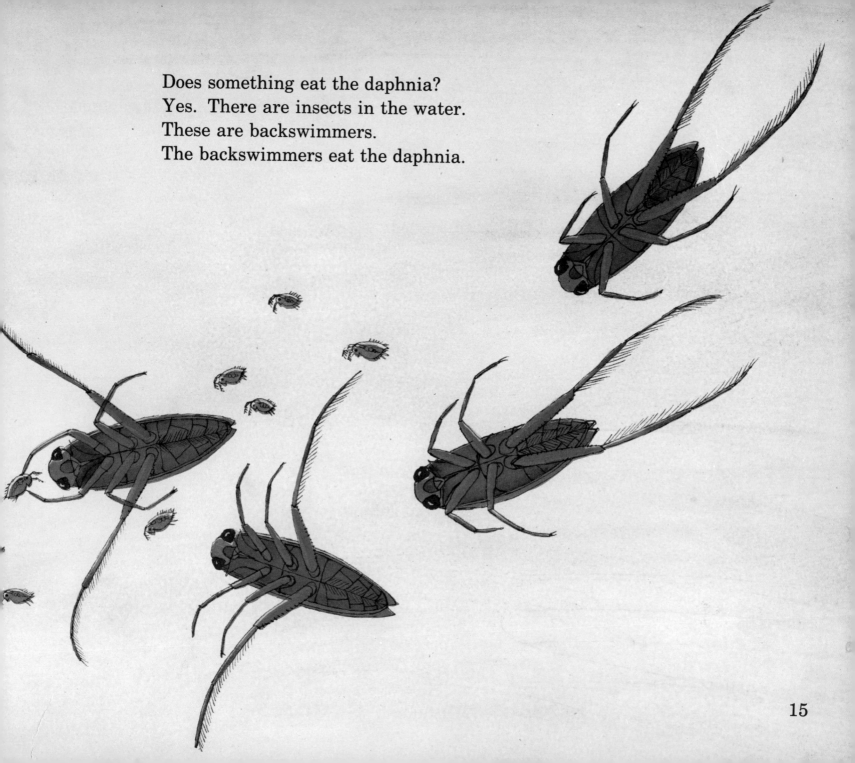

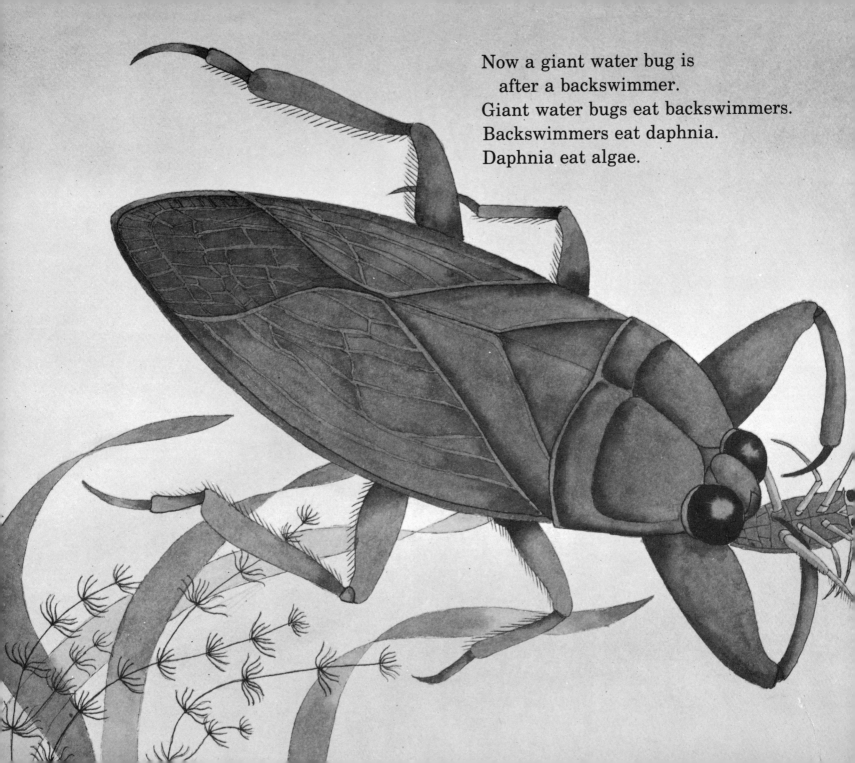

Now a giant water bug is
  after a backswimmer.
Giant water bugs eat backswimmers.
Backswimmers eat daphnia.
Daphnia eat algae.

The giant water bug, backswimmers, daphnia,
and algae make a food chain.

A frog eats the giant water bug.
So the frog must be part of the food chain, too.
Another giant water bug is going
    after some little sunfish.
It catches one of the sunfish.

19

Is the sunfish part of this chain?
No, I think the sunfish is part of another food chain.
Well, then, what does a sunfish eat?
Here are some snails.
They eat algae.
And look! A sunfish eats one of the snails!

The frog, the giant water bug, backswimmers,
    daphnia, and algae make one food chain.
And the giant water bug, sunfish, snail,
    and algae make another chain.
The frog and the giant water bug are in two chains.
The two chains make a food web.

One giant water bug ate
    a backswimmer.
That was part of one food chain.
And a giant water bug ate
    a sunfish in another chain.
An animal may eat things
    from many chains.
Then it is part of a big food web.

Some webs have just two chains.
Some have many.
Hey, look. There is the hawk again!
What is it after now?
A snake! And the snake has the frog!

Now the hawk dives!
The hawk catches the snake.
And the snake lets the frog go.
The frog splashes into the water.

The hawk is part of a very big food web.
There are many chains in that web.
One chain is the hawk, snake, frog, giant
water bug, sunfish, snail, and algae.
The hawk ate a mouse, too.
The mouse was part of another chain.
And the blackbird and the muskrat?
Yes, they are parts of other food chains.

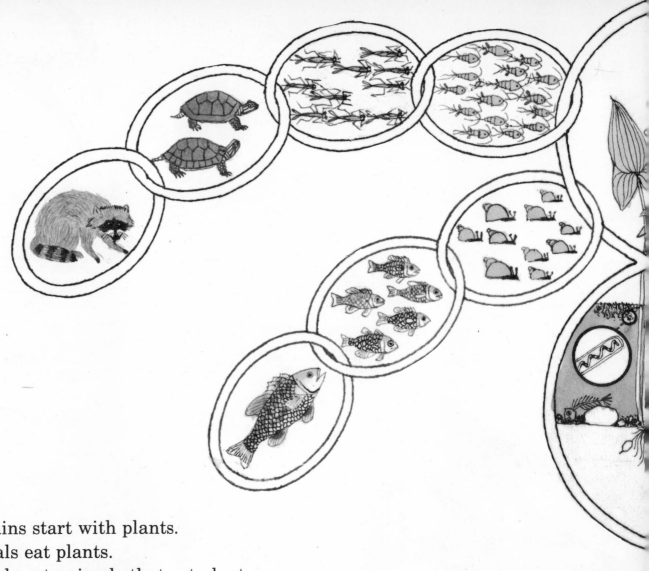

All food chains start with plants.
Some animals eat plants.
Some animals eat animals that eat plants.
Some food chains are very long.
But they all go back to plants.

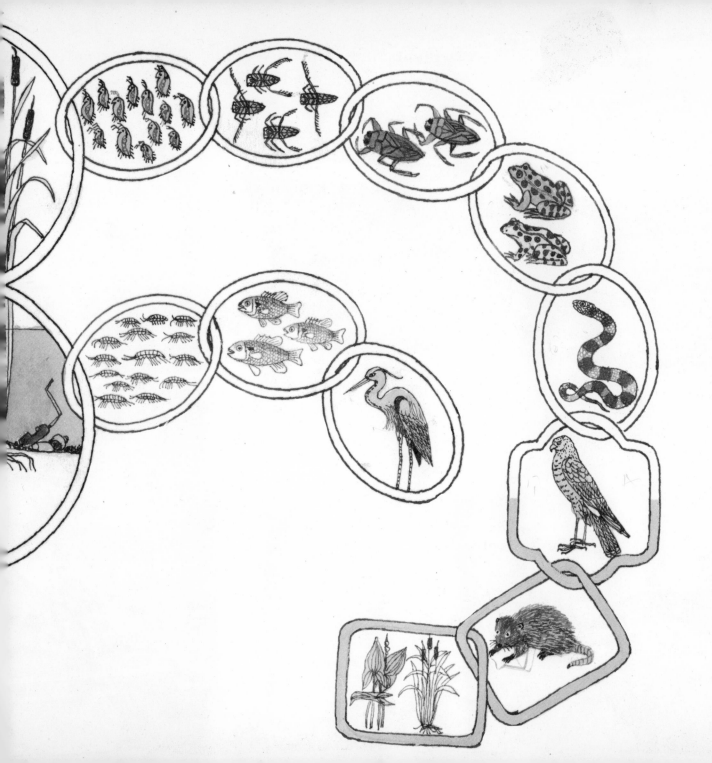

Plants and animals — is that all animals eat?
Well, there is dead stuff, too.

Some of it comes from dead plants.
Some of it comes from dead animals.
The dead stuff is called detritus.
Look down there, under the water.
See that black stuff?
That is detritus.

Do animals eat that black stuff?
Yes, some of them do.
Animals that eat detritus are called scavengers.
See the crayfish down there?
Crayfish are scavengers.

Many little animals are scavengers, too.
Some of them are scuds.
Scuds eat the detritus.
Many other things live on detritus.
Some are so very little we cannot see them.

crayfish

32

Bigger animals eat the scuds.
Bigger animals eat crayfish, too.
So some food chains start with detritus.
But detritus comes from dead plants and dead animals.
So detritus chains start with plants, too.

scuds

Hey! I think I have a fish!
Look at that!
A big sunfish! Look at it splash!

You know something?
I think we are part of a food chain, too.
We are going to eat this sunfish.
And the sunfish ate the snails.
And the snails ate the algae.
We eat many other things, too.
We must be part of a big food web!
We eat animal food.
And we eat plant food, too.

Our day is about over.
We must go home soon.
We can come back tomorrow.
Maybe we will see the hawk again.
Maybe we will see some animals
  we did not see today.
And maybe we will catch a bigger fish!

39

About the Authors

Herbert H. Wong is well known as an author of science books for children and teachers, as a science education consultant, and as an educator. He is the Principal of the University of California Laboratory School, Washington Elementary, in Berkeley, California. Dr. Wong is active in many current science curriculum development projects and pilot programs. He holds a degree in Zoology and the Ed.D. from the University of California.

Matthew F. Vessel, Associate Dean of the School of Natural Science and Mathematics of San Jose State College, is an author, editor, and consultant, in science and education. He is a Fellow of the American Association for the Advancement of Science. An active member of many other professional science and education societies, Dr. Vessel attended St. Cloud Teachers College and the University of Minnesota. He holds the Ph.D. from Cornell University.

About the Artist

Tony Chen's interest in animals dates from his childhood in Jamaica. At one time he had a collection of seven pets that were on the order of a personal zoo. He is still an avid collector. Only, now Mr. Chen specializes in the arts of early-dynastic China, and primitive sculpture from diverse cultures. Most of the works, of course, represent animals. A *cum laude* graduate of the Pratt Institute, Mr. Chen is an Account Art Director for *Newsweek*. Many of his paintings, water colors and pieces of sculpture are in private collections.